Science
Vocabulary Readers

Ladybug
Life Cycle

Justin McCory Martin

SCHOLASTIC INC.

NEW YORK • TORONTO • LONDON • AUCKLAND • SYDNEY
MEXICO CITY • NEW DELHI • HONG KONG • BUENOS AIRES

ISBN-13: 978-0-439-87656-8 / ISBN-10: 0-439-87656-7

Photos Credits:
Cover: © Phone Labat Jean-Michel/Peter Arnold, Inc.; title page: © Stephen Dalton/Minden Pictures; contents page, from top: © Stephen Dalton/Minden Pictures, © Hans Pfletschinger/Peter Arnold Inc., © Getty Images, © Cisco Castelijns/Foto Natura/Minden; page 4: © Stephen Dalton/Minden Pictures; page 5: Getty Images; page 6: © Bruce Coleman USA Inc.; page 6, inset: © Jef Meul/Foto Natura/Minden; page 7: © Stephen Dalton/Minden Pictures; page 8: © Hans Pfletschinger/Peter Arnold Inc.; page 9: © Dwight Kuhn Photography; page 10: © Stephen Dalton/Minden Pictures; page 10, inset: © Volker Steger/Photo Researchers, Inc.; page 11: © Bruce Coleman USA Inc.; page 11, inset: © Bruce Coleman USA Inc.; page 12: © Getty Images; page 13: © Getty Images; page 14: © Getty Images; page 14, inset: © Bruce Coleman USA Inc.; page 15: © Kim Taylor/Nature Picture Library; page 16, left: © Hans Pfletschinger/Peter Arnold Inc.; page 16, right: © Bruce Coleman USA Inc.; page 17, left: © Getty Images; page 17, right: © Getty Images; page 18, left: © Stephen Dalton/Minden Pictures; page 18, right: Bruce Coleman USA Inc.; page 19, top left: © Cisco Castelijns/Foto Natura/Minden; page 19, top right © Meul/ARCO/Nature Picture Library; page 19 bottom; © Bruce Coleman USA Inc.; page 20: © Anthony Bannister/Gallo Images/Corbis; page 20, inset: © Jef Meul/Foto Natura/Minden Pictures; page 21: © Buddy Mays/Corbis: ©; page 22: © Getty Images; page 24: © Jef Meul/Foto Natura/Minden Pictures; back cover: © Hans Pfletschinger/Peter Arnold Inc.

Photo research by Dwayne Howard
Design by Holly Grundon

12 11 10 9 8 7 6 5 4   8 9 10 11 12/0

Printed in the U.S.A.
First printing, March 2007

Contents

Chapter 1

All About Ladybugs

What is tiny, shiny, and dressed in a spotted coat? A ladybug!

Ladybugs are insects. They are part of a group of insects called **beetles**.

Ladybug Parts

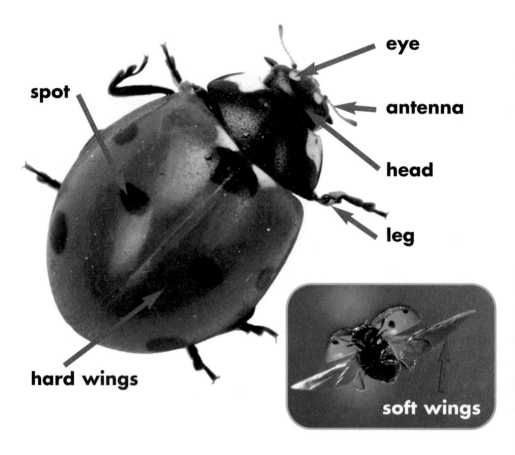

spot

eye

antenna

head

leg

hard wings

soft wings

Ladybugs have six legs and two pairs of wings. One pair of wings is hard. They protect another pair of wings that is **fragile** and used for flying.

Fast Fact

Ladybugs use their antennae (an-**ten**-ee) **to feel, smell, and taste.**

But ladybugs do not begin their lives looking this way at all. Read on to learn about the life cycle of this incredible bug.

Chapter 2

Egg to Larva

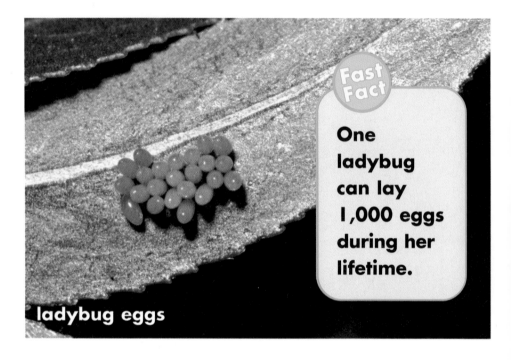

Fast Fact

One ladybug can lay 1,000 eggs during her lifetime.

ladybug eggs

A ladybug starts life inside an egg. Females lay eggs on leaves. The eggs look like teeny, yellow jellybeans.

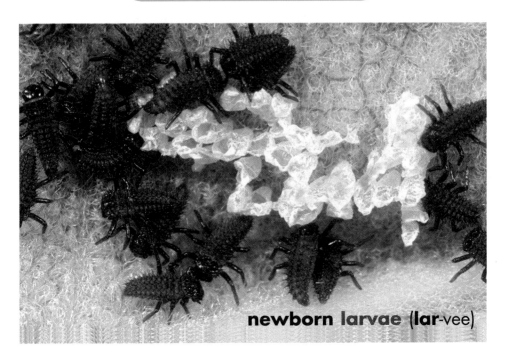

newborn **larvae** (**lar**-vee)

A few days later, the eggs hatch and out crawl tiny creatures. These are ladybug larvae. Munch! Munch! They are so hungry they eat their own eggshells.

An aphid looks like this close up.

The job of a larva is to eat, eat, eat! Its favorite food is a teeny bug called an aphid. A larva can eat 25 aphids in one day.

A larva grows to be about this big.

growing ladybug larva

All that eating makes the larva grow and grow! It may not look like a ladybug yet, but just wait. Something amazing is about to happen.

Chapter 3

Pupa to Little Ladybug

ladybug pupa

After a few weeks, the larva stops moving and attaches itself to a leaf. Then it turns into something called a pupa. A pupa is like a wrapped-up present.

A ladybug is born!

Guess what happens next? About one week later, the pupa breaks open. Surprise! Out pops a little ladybug.

An adult ladybug is about this size. That is smaller than the larva it came from!

At first, the ladybug is soft and pale. But after a few hours its shell gets hard and bright like this.

A ladybug flies to a flower.

Soon the ladybug is able to spread its wings and fly. Wow! At last, it is all grown-up.

Life Cycle Review

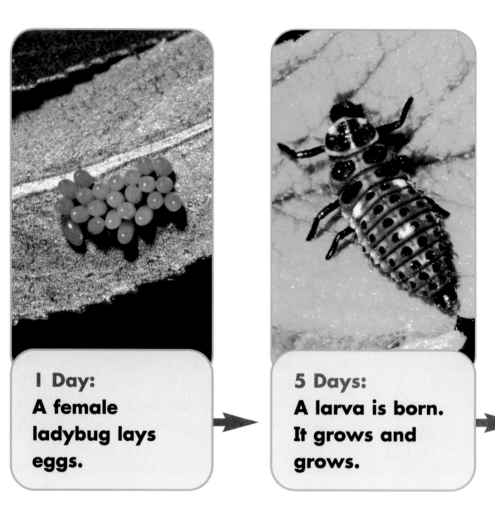

1 Day:
A female ladybug lays eggs.

5 Days:
A larva is born. It grows and grows.

Ladybugs have a very interesting life cycle. Do you remember the four main steps?

25 Days:
A larva turns into a pupa.

32 Days:
A pupa turns into a ladybug.

The life cycle of most ladybugs takes four to six weeks.

Chapter 4

All Grown-up!

There are more than 4,000 kinds of ladybugs in the world. Some are red with a few spots. Some are red with lots of spots!

Fast Fact

Ladybugs have zero to 24 spots. How many spots do these have?

Some ladybugs are brown or gold. Some are even sunny yellow!

Fast Fact

Ladybugs eat the pollen of flowers, too.

During the summer, ladybugs eat lots of aphids and small insects. Munch! Munch! They want to have full stomachs for the long winter ahead. Why?

A group of ladybugs hibernate.

Many kinds of ladybugs hibernate. They gather in groups. Then they hide under leaves, rocks, or logs to sleep all winter.

In spring, the ladybugs wake up and the females lay eggs. After that, the incredible ladybug life cycle starts all over again!

Glossary

antennae (an-**ten**-ee): the two feelers on top of a bug's head

aphid (**ay**-fid): a tiny bug eaten by ladybugs

beetle (**bee**-tuhl): a type of insect with two pairs of wings

fragile (**fraj**-il): easy to break

hibernate (**hye**-bur-nate): to go into a deep sleep that lasts through the winter

larvae (**lar**-vee): insects at the stage of development between egg and pupa; a single insect at this stage is called a larva

pollen (**pol**-uhn): tiny yellow grains made by flowers

pupa (**pyoo**-puh): the stage in an insect's life right before it becomes an adult

Comprehension Questions

1. Can you name four parts of a ladybug?

2. Can you retell the four main steps of a ladybug's life cycle?

3. Can you name four colors that ladybugs come in?

4. Can you think of four words to describe a ladybug?

Bonus Fast Facts

- Ladybugs live for about one year.

- Ladybugs flap their wings 85 times a second when they fly.

- Ladybugs sometimes play dead when they are scared.